LOS ANGELES RAMS

BY JOSH ANDERSON

Stride
An Imprint of The Child's World®
childsworld.com

The Child's World®
childsworld.com

Published by The Child's World®
800-599-READ • www.childsworld.com

Photography Credits
Cover: © Christian Petersen / Staff / Getty Images; page 1: © Africa Studio / Shutterstock; page 3: © Thearon W. Henderson / Stringer / Getty Images; page 5: © Katelyn Mulcahy / Stringer / Getty Images; page 6: © Staff / Getty Images; page 9: © Brian Bahr / Staff / Getty Images; page 10: © Katelyn Mulcahy / Stringer / Getty Images; page 11: © stevezmina1 / Getty Images; page 12: © Sean M. Haffey / Staff / Getty Images; page 12: © Harry How / Staff / Getty Images; page 13: © Ronald Martinez / Staff / Getty Images; page 13: © Jayne Kamin-Oncea / Stringer / Getty Images; page 14: © Katelyn Mulcahy / Stringer / Getty Images; page 15: © Martin Leitch/Icon Sportswire / Newscom; page 16: © Otto Greule Jr / Stringer / Getty Images; page 16: © Rick Stewart / Stringer / Getty Images; page 17: © David Durochik / Associated Press; page 17: © Scott Halleran / Staff / Getty Images; page 18: © Hale, Fraser/St. Petersburg Times / Newscom; page 18: © Andy Lyons / Staff / Getty Images; page 19: © Harry How / Staff / Getty Images; page 19: © John W. McDonough/SI/Icon SMI / Newscom; page 20: © Katelyn Mulcahy / Stringer / Getty Images; page 20: © Ronald Martinez / Staff / Getty Images; page 21: © Ronald Martinez / Staff / Getty Images; page 21: © Ezra Shaw / Staff / Getty Images; page 22: © Tony Tomsic / SportsChrome / Newscom; page 23: © George Rose / Stringer / Getty Images; page 23: © stevezmina1 / Getty Images; page 25: © Andy Lyons / Staff / Getty Images; page 26: © Sean M. Haffey / Staff / Getty Images; page 29: © Tim DeFrisco / Stringer / Getty Images

ISBN Information
9781503857902 (Reinforced Library Binding)
9781503860551 (Portable Document Format)
9781503861916 (Online Multi-user eBook)
9781503863279 (Electronic Publication)

LCCN 2021952632

Printed in the United States of America

BRINGING THE WORLD TO YOUNG READERS 1968

TABLE OF CONTENTS

Go Rams! 4
Becoming the Rams 6
By the Numbers 8
Game Day 10
Uniform 12
Team Spirit 14
Heroes of History 16
Big Days 18
Modern-Day Marvels 20
The GOAT 22
The Big Game 24
Amazing Feats 26
All-Time Best 28

Glossary 30
Find Out More 31
Index and About the Author 32

GO RAMS!

The Los Angeles Rams compete in the National Football **League's** (NFL's) National Football Conference (NFC). They play in the NFC West **division**, along with the Arizona Cardinals, San Francisco 49ers, and Seattle Seahawks. Many Rams fans in California were thrilled when the team moved back to Los Angeles in 2016 after 21 seasons in St. Louis, Missouri. The team even made it to the **Super Bowl** for the first time since 2001 in their third season back in Los Angeles. Three years later, they won the big game after an amazing 2021 season. Let's learn more about the Rams!

NFC WEST DIVISION

Arizona Cardinals

Los Angeles Rams

San Francisco 49ers

Seattle Seahawks

WIDE RECEIVER COOPER KUPP (LEFT) LED THE NFL WITH 16 RECEIVING TOUCHDOWNS IN 2021.

BECOMING THE RAMS

The Rams began play in Cleveland, Ohio, in 1937. They spent eight seasons in their original home and won the NFL Championship in their last year in Cleveland. In 1946, the team moved to Los Angeles, California. The Rams became the first top-level professional sports team ever to be located on the West Coast of the United States. The team left Los Angeles in 1995 for St. Louis, Missouri, but returned in 2016. The Rams brought glory to the city of Los Angeles following the 2021 season when they won Super Bowl 56 in their home stadium.

VINCE FERRAGAMO STARTED 44 GAMES FOR THE RAMS IN THE LATE 1970S AND EARLY 1980S.

BY THE NUMBERS

The Rams have won **TWO** Super Bowls.

22 division titles for the Rams

540 points for the Rams in 2000—a team record!

14 wins for the Rams in 2001

THE RAMS WON THE FIRST SUPER BOWL OF THIS MILLENNIUM IN JANUARY 2000.

SOFI IS ONE OF THE NFL'S NEWEST STADIUMS.

GAME DAY

For most of their years in Los Angeles, the Rams played their home games at Los Angeles Memorial Coliseum. The building hosted the 1932 and 1984 Summer Olympics and is a National Historic Landmark. In 2020, the Rams moved into a brand-new building, SoFi **Stadium**. SoFi is also home to the NFL's Los Angeles Chargers. On game days, SoFi Stadium holds a little more than 70,000 fans. The stadium is covered by a clear plastic roof that lets in plenty of light.

We're Famous!

There was once a movie about a Rams backup quarterback accidentally going to heaven! The 1978 movie *Heaven Can Wait* includes a scene in which the film's main character plays in the Super Bowl. The movie's Super Bowl was actually filmed during the halftime of a Rams preseason game against the San Diego Chargers. Several retired Rams players appear in the movie.

UNIFORM

Truly Weird

The Rams were expected to win their 2021 game against the Detroit Lions, but the Lions had tricks up their sleeves. After Detroit scored a **touchdown** on their opening drive, they used a surprise **onside kick** to get the football back and kick a field goal. The Rams were down 10–0 before they ever had the ball! The Lions used two fake punts later in the game. The trick plays helped keep the Lions close, but the Rams went on to win 28–19.

Alternate Jersey

Sometimes teams wear an alternate jersey that is different from their home and away jerseys. It might be a bright color or have a unique theme. The Rams wore all-gold uniforms for a Monday Night Football game against the Baltimore Ravens in 2019. The new look proved unlucky, though. The Rams lost 45–6.

PLAYERS ENTER SOFI STADIUM THROUGH TWO GIANT RAMS' HEADS BEFORE HOME GAMES.

TEAM SPIRIT

Going to a game at SoFi Stadium can be loads of fun. Before the game, fans can tailgate, which means enjoying food and drink brought from home in the stadium's parking lot. Inside SoFi Stadium, the Los Angeles Rams Cheerleaders entertain fans at every home game. The team's mascot, Rampage, has been cheering on the team since 2010. He's a giant costumed Ram who wears a team jersey, just like the players. Hungry fans at SoFi should not miss the stadium's tsunami tots, crispy tater tots topped with eel sauce, mayonnaise, and sriracha.

RAMPAGE

HEROES OF HISTORY

Isaac Bruce

Wide Receiver | 1994–2007

Bruce ranks fifth all-time with 15,208 receiving yards. He also ranks 13th all-time with 91 touchdown receptions. He led the NFL in receiving in 1996 when he finished with 1,338 yards. Bruce was selected for four **Pro Bowls** and is a member of the Pro Football **Hall of Fame**.

Eric Dickerson

Running Back | 1983–1987

Dickerson led the NFL in rushing during three of his four full seasons with the Rams. For his career, Dickerson ranks ninth all-time with 13,259 rushing yards. He also ranks 13th all-time with 90 rushing touchdowns. Dickerson is a member of the Pro Football Hall of Fame.

Merlin Olsen

Defensive Tackle | 1962–1976

No one has been selected to more Pro Bowls in a row than Merlin Olsen. Olsen was honored with selection after each of the first 14 seasons of his career. He was part of the "Fearsome Foursome" defensive line for the 1960s Rams. Olsen was picked for the Pro Football Hall of Fame in 1982.

Kurt Warner

Quarterback | 1998–2003

Warner led the Rams to victory in Super Bowl 34 against the Tennessee Titans. He was chosen as the NFL's **Most Valuable Player** in 1999 and 2001. In 2001, he led the NFL in completion percentage, passing yards, and passing touchdowns. He's a member of the Pro Football Hall of Fame.

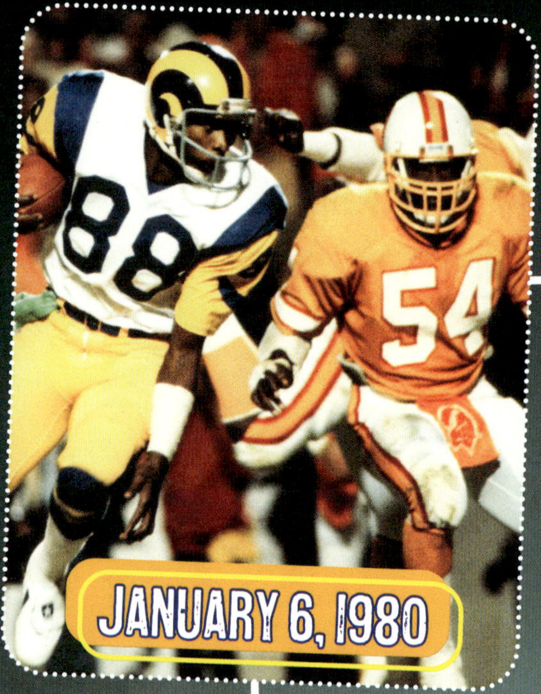

JANUARY 6, 1980

The Rams defeat the Tampa Bay Buccaneers in the NFC Championship Game and earn their first-ever trip to the Super Bowl.

JANUARY 30, 2000

The Rams defeat the Tennessee Titans 23–16 in Super Bowl 34.

BIG DAYS

SEPTEMBER 18, 2016

The Rams defeat the Philadelphia Eagles and win their second NFC Championship in three years.

SEPTEMBER 18, 2016

In their first home game in Los Angeles since 1994, the Rams defeat the Seattle Seahawks 9–3.

MODERN-DAY MARVELS

Aaron Donald

Defensive Lineman | Debut: 2014

Donald was chosen as the NFL's Defensive Player of the Year in 2017, 2018, and 2020. He's been chosen for the Pro Bowl every season of his career. In 2018, he led the NFL with 20.5 **sacks**, the eighth most ever in a single season.

Cooper Kupp

Wide Receiver | Debut: 2017

Kupp registered his first 1,000-yard season in 2019. In 2021, he had 145 receptions for 1,947 yards and 16 touchdowns, leading the league in all three categories. Kupp was chosen for his first Pro Bowl after the 2021 season.

Jalen Ramsey

Cornerback | Debut: 2019

In college, Ramsey starred at Florida State University. As a pro, he was traded from the Jacksonville Jaguars to the Rams during the 2019 NFL season. Ramsey was chosen for the Pro Bowl in five of his first six seasons. He helped the Rams finish with the league's top-ranked defense in 2020.

Matthew Stafford

Quarterback | Debut: 2021

Stafford was picked first overall by the Detroit Lions in the 2009 NFL Draft. He was traded to the Rams before the 2021 season and led the team to the Super Bowl. Stafford ranks in the top 15 all-time in completed passes, passing yards, and passing touchdowns. He was chosen for the Pro Bowl in 2014.

DEACON JONES PLAYED 11 OF HIS 14 NFL SEASONS FOR THE RAMS.

THE GOAT

GREATEST OF ALL TIME

DEACON JONES

Jones struck fear in the hearts of opposing quarterbacks. He was the first ever to use the term *sack* for when he tackled a quarterback behind the line of scrimmage. Although sacks were not an official NFL statistic until 1982, Jones ranks third all-time on the list of unofficial leaders with 173.5. He was picked for seven-straight Pro Bowls from 1964 to 1970. Jones was elected to the Pro Football Hall of Fame in 1980. He was also chosen for the NFL's 100th Anniversary All-Time Team.

FAN FAVORITE

#1

Jackie Slater–Offensive Tackle

1976–1995

Slater's talent as an offensive lineman was matched only by the length of his career. Slater made seven Pro Bowls and is one of the most beloved Rams ever because he spent two full decades with the team. Slater's long career was honored when he became a member of the Pro Football Hall of Fame in 2001.

THE BIG GAME

FEB. 13, 2022 - SUPER BOWL 56

The Rams' opponents in Super Bowl 56 were the Cincinnati Bengals. The game was played at SoFi Stadium, the Rams' home field. Los Angeles took the lead in the first quarter on a touchdown pass from Matthew Stafford to Odell Beckham Jr. The Rams held the lead until just after halftime when the Bengals went ahead 13–10. It wasn't until Cooper Kupp caught a one-yard touchdown pass with less than two minutes to play that the Rams took the lead again. Los Angeles held on for a 23–20 victory, giving the Rams their second Super Bowl victory in team history.

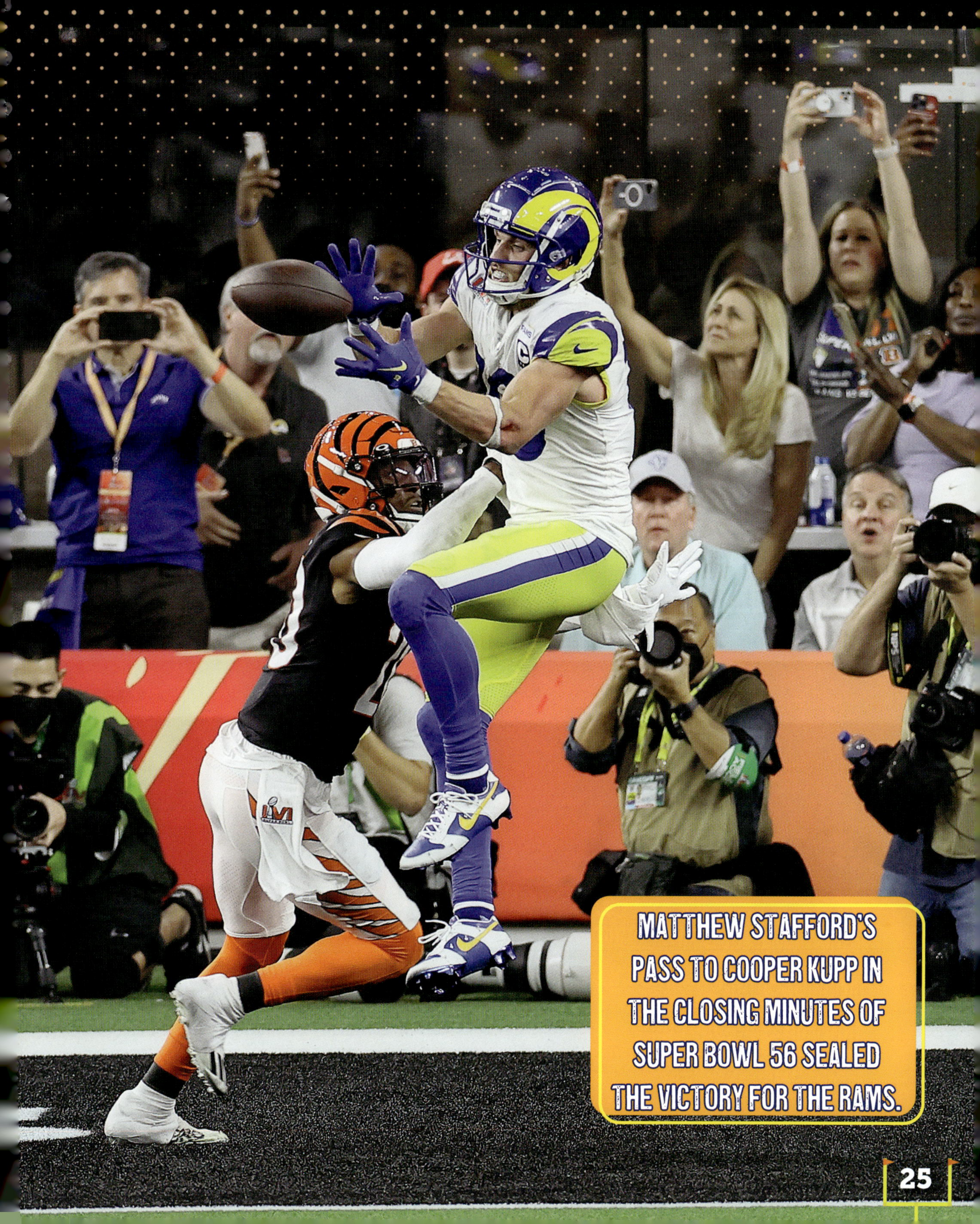

MATTHEW STAFFORD'S PASS TO COOPER KUPP IN THE CLOSING MINUTES OF SUPER BOWL 56 SEALED THE VICTORY FOR THE RAMS.

SEAN MCVAY LED THE RAMS TO A 13-3 RECORD IN 2018, AND THE TEAM EARNED A TRIP TO THE SUPER BOWL.

AMAZING FEATS

4,886 Passing Yards

In 2021 by
QUARTERBACK
Matthew Stafford

18 Rushing Touchdowns

In 2000 by
RUNNING BACK
Marshall Faulk

17 Touchdown Catches

In 1951 by
WIDE RECEIVER
Elroy Hirsch

14 Interceptions

In 1952 by
CORNERBACK
Dick "Night Train" Lane

ALL-TIME BEST

PASSING YARDS

Jim Everett
23,758

Marc Bulger
22,814

Roman Gabriel
22,223

RUSHING YARDS

Steven Jackson
10,138

Eric Dickerson
7,245

Marshall Faulk
6,959

RECEIVING YARDS

Isaac Bruce
14,109

Torry Holt
12,660

Henry Ellard
9,761

SACKS**

Deacon Jones
159.5

Jack Youngblood
151.5

Aaron Donald
98*

SCORING

Jeff Wilkins
1,223

Greg Zuerlein
867

Mike Lansford
789

INTERCEPTIONS

Eddie Meador
46

Nolan Cromwell
37

LeRoy Irvin
34

*as of 2021
**unofficial before 1982

JIM EVERETT LED THE RAMS TO THE NFC CHAMPIONSHIP GAME AFTER THE 1989 NFL SEASON.

GLOSSARY

division (dih-VIZSH-un): a group of teams within the NFL who play each other more frequently and compete for the best record

Hall of Fame (HALL of FAYM): a museum in Canton, Ohio, that honors the best players in NFL history

league (LEEG): an organization of sports teams that compete against each other

Most Valuable Player (MOHST VALL-yuh-bul PLAY-uhr): a yearly award given to the top player in the NFL

onside kick (AHN-syd KIK): a short kickoff meant to give the kicking team a chance to recover the football

Pro Bowl (PRO BOWL): the NFL's All-Star game, where the best players in the league compete

sack (SAK): when a quarterback is tackled behind the line of scrimmage before he can throw the ball

stadium (STAY-dee-uhm): a building with a field and seats for fans where teams play

Super Bowl (SOO-puhr BOWL): the championship game of the NFL, played between the winners of the AFC and the NFC

touchdown (TUTCH-down): a play in which the ball is brought into the other team's end zone, resulting in six points

FIND OUT MORE

IN THE LIBRARY

Bulgar, Beth and Mark Bechtel. *My First Book of Football.* New York, NY: Time Inc. Books, 2015.

Jacobs, Greg. *The Everything Kids' Football Book, 7th Edition*. Avon, MA: Adams Media, 2021.

Sports Illustrated Kids. *The Greatest Football Teams of All Time*. New York, NY: Time Inc. Books, 2018.

Wyner, Zach. *Los Angeles Rams*. New York, NY: AV2, 2020.

ON THE WEB

Visit our website for links about the Los Angeles Rams:
childsworld.com/links

Note to parents, teachers, and librarians: We routinely verify our web links to make sure they are safe and active sites. Encourage your readers to check them out!

INDEX

Beckham, Odell, Jr. 24
Bruce, Isaac 16, 28

Dickerson, Eric 16, 28
Donald, Aaron 20, 28

Jones, Deacon 22–23, 28

Kupp, Cooper 5, 20, 24–25
McVay, Sean 26

National Football Conference (NFC) 4, 18–19, 29
NFL Championship 7
NFL Draft 21

Olsen, Merlin 17

Rampage 15
Ramsey, Jalen 21

Slater, Jackie 23
SoFi Stadium 10–11, 14–15, 24
Stafford, Matthew 21, 24–25, 27
Super Bowl 4, 7–9, 11, 17–18, 21, 24–26

Warner, Kurt 17

ABOUT THE AUTHOR

Josh Anderson has published over 50 books for children and young adults. His two boys are the greatest joys in his life. Hobbies include coaching his sons in youth basketball, no-holds-barred games of Apples to Apples, and taking long family walks. His favorite NFL team is a secret he'll never share!